YES, I HAVE TIME

Transforming Lives Through Christian Counseling

Timothy Ware Sr.

Copyright © 2020 by Timothy Ware Sr.

All rights reserved. No part of this publication may be reproduced, distributed or transmitted in any form or by any means, including photocopying, recording, or other electronic or mechanical methods, without the prior written permission of the publisher, except in the case of brief quotations embodied in critical reviews and certain other noncommercial uses permitted by copyright law. For permission requests, write to the publisher, addressed "Attention: Permissions Coordinator," at the address below.

Ken Cox /Rejoice Essential Publishing
PO BOX 512
Effingham, SC 29541
www.republishing.org

Unless otherwise indicated, scriptures are taken from the King James Version.

Scripture quotations marked HCSB are taken from the Holman Christian Standard Bible®, Used by Permission HCSB ©1999,2000,2002,2003,2009 Holman Bible Publishers. Holman Christian Standard Bible®, Holman CSB®, and HCSB® are federally registered trademarks of Holman Bible Publishers.

"The Scriptures quoted are from the NET Bible® http://netbible.com copyright ©1996, 2019 used with permission from Biblical Studies Press, L.L.C. All rights reserved".

Scripture quotations marked (NIV) are taken from the Holy Bible, New International Version®, NIV®. Copyright © 1973, 1978, 1984, 2011 by Biblica, Inc.™ Used by permission of Zondervan. All rights reserved worldwide. www.zondervan.comThe "NIV" and "New International Version" are trademarks registered in the United States Patent and Trademark Office by Biblica, Inc.™

Yes, I Have Time/Timothy Ware Sr.
ISBN-13: 978-1-952312-39-7
Library of Congress Control Number: 2020920701

Dedication

I dedicate this book to anyone that is feeling down, depressed, and like everyone and everything is against them. I feel your pain because I was once that person. I wrote this book for you, but never in my wildest imagination would I envision a nation of people in disarray. We are in an hour where many no longer have the time to encourage others, counsel the troubled mind, or change someone's life through Scripture, prayer, and counseling. This book is for you. Yes, I have time for you. The varying manifestations of God's tremendous healing power as Jehovah-Rapha can be found in this book.

Acknowledgments

Those of you who have a counseling or psychology degree, especially those who have professional practices, know that many counselors and psychologists are responsible for getting a finished and comprehensive book into the reading audience's hands. This book, in particular, was birthed as the result of hard work and academic success (graduating magna cum laude and summa cum laude). The book's richness and value reveal the expert knowledge that many of my collegiate professors have poured into me.

I would be remiss if I did not honor and thank my mom, Betty J. Ware. It is because of your fervent prayers that I'm the saved and productive man I am today. Thank you to all my siblings as well as my immediate family. Also, I would love to thank Prophetess Kimberly Moses and her awesome publishing company, Rejoice Essential Publishing, for believing in me and publishing this book. Thanks to your amazing gifts, you were able to capture my literary vision in the creative designing of the book.

My heart and great thanks are given to my beautiful wife, Dr. Zolisha L. Ware, for her continuous support. Special thanks to you, Pastors Joseph and Vickie Brown, for your inspiration and Godly leadership. And thank you, Timothy Ware Jr., Shantel Moore, and Kalin Ware, my treasured children, for your support and long-suffering. Thank you, always, for all the love and patience that you all have poured into my life and this book.

Foreword

BECOMING AWARE

As a Christian, I learned early on that for every natural problem and situation, there is a spiritual answer. Therefore, whether I'm facilitating a Moral Reconation Therapy group for the McLean County Probation Department, teaching a criminology class for Heartland Community College, or serving as a McLean County Youthbuild Board member, I do my best to see things through the lens of God and practice His principles.

The Bible proclaims that: Jesus is the way, the truth, and the life; in the beginning, was the Word, and the Word was with God, and the Word was God; seek ye first the kingdom of God and his righteousness, and we are to be transformed by the renewing of our minds. Christians follow the Word of God because it is the truth that defines good character, makes us aware of our mistakes, delivers us from ourselves, and helps us to become new. Because if we live the Word, old things are passed away, and all things about us become new, making us new creatures in Christ.

In addition to serving as a probation officer for thirty-three years, college professor for twenty-four years, and McLean County Youthbuild Board member for twenty-four years, I've been serving the Lord since 1985 and preaching the gospel for twenty-five years. I truly believe that faith without works is dead, I should submit my body a living sacrifice, and sin is what separates man from God. I've watched the life of Deacon Timothy Ware, and not only does he believe in these precepts, but by example, he has taught me what it really means to serve people and be committed to the Lord.

If you have not given your life to the Lord, or you are a Christian who needs spiritual guidance, I urge you to consider *Yes, I Have Time: Transforming Lives Through Christian Counseling*. If you need confidence, better communication skills, knowledge of how to better your marital relationship, *Yes, I Have Time: Transforming Lives Through Christian Counseling* will make you aware of the steps that are necessary to go from faith to faith, glory to glory, and victory to victory in the aforementioned areas and more. Based on his life experiences and years of service to the Lord, Timothy Ware, an astute preacher of the gospel, will make you aware of what you need to prosper and be in good health even as your soul prospers.

Elder/Professor Dewhitt Lloyd Bingham

Contents

ACKNOWLEDGMENTS..v
FOREWORD..viii
CHAPTER ONE: Introduction to
    Christian Counseling......................................1
CHAPTER TWO: Basic Counseling Skills
    & Technique...5
    Effective Communicator................................7
    Active and Empathic Listener........................8
    Ethical and Trustworthy................................9
    Spiritual Maturity...10
CHAPTER THREE: Change Your Mindset,
    Transform Your Life....................................13
    Behavior Therapy...15
    Behavior Therapy and Christian
    Counseling...17
CHAPTER FOUR: Counseling in Times
    of Trouble..21
    HOPE: Helping Our People Exceed............24
CHAPTER FIVE: Rekindle the Passion
    in your Marriage..28
    Triangular Theory of Love...........................31
    The Color Wheel Model of Love.................33
    Enhancing Marital Intimacy Through
    Facilitating Cognitive Self-Disclosure.........34

  Sound Relationship House Theory..............35
CHAPTER SIX: Dealing with Addiction................40
  Counseling Addiction................................43
CHAPTER SEVEN: Teach Me How to
  Forgive...47
  Importance of Forgiveness in
  Relationships..48
  Letting Go of Resentment..........................50
  Forgiveness and Reconciliation in
  Relationships..51
  Application..56
ABOUT THE AUTHOR...60
BIBLIOGRAPHY 61

Chapter One

Introduction to Christian Counseling

"But the Counselor, the Holy Spirit–the Father will send Him in My name–will teach you all things and remind you of everything I have told you." (John 14:26 HCSB)

This chapter is a general introduction to Christian counseling, including an overview of current trends in counseling theories and practices, as well as the role of the Christian counselor in public, private, and church settings. So, there are no misunderstandings, this author acknowledges the simple fact that Christian counseling differs from secular counseling.

First of all, Christian counselors are mostly Christian by faith not necessarily by merely practice. The reason for this is because we genuinely want to help clients grow closer to God and understand what His will is for their life and any problem they have encountered. In general, all problems and all issues and all situations are addressed directly by the Scripture itself. Empowered by the Holy Spirit, it is seen as the source, the means, and the foundation where we find the purpose of Christian counseling.

As Christians, especially Christian counselors, we have a debt to pay out of our gratitude for what Jesus Christ has done for us. His crucifixion, death, and resurrection made way for all of us to receive God's grace, redemption, and forgiveness. We have been entrusted with the task of teaching salvation and redemption; and in return, we pray that God will qualify and instruct the client to teach others (2 Timothy 2:1-2). Also, practicing what Apostle Paul calls mutual faith, which means encouragement, support, and our spiritual gifts, all working collectively together to inspire, encourage, correct, and instruct one another (Ephesians 4:15-16).

The Christian counselor must also be a student of God's word because Christian counseling involves the therapeutic application of empathetic listening, discernment, practical knowledge, and the careful application of the Word of God directly or indirectly to every situation presented to the counselor. Because competent Christian counseling demands that we move beyond simple sin management and behavior modifications. We need to tap into our God-given talent, which is the Holy Spirit, so we can effectively counsel and minster. The heart of effective Christian counseling is knowing how to use your skills and techniques to create the right spiritual environment that facilitates lasting change and transformation.

There are several other skills and characteristics that can be found in a great Christian counselor, such as, the ability to empathetically communicate and listen. People expect to be listened to with compassion and cared for with godly love. Since most clients may not know what Christian counseling will look like or how it will benefit them, the counselor-counselee relationship must be trustworthy, Scripture-based, and Christ-centered. Scripture-based and Christ-centered counseling is a much-needed resource that will set a frame of reference for your existing Christian counseling ministry. It is also vital that the Pastor take seriously the call to correct and rebuke their congregants through Christ-centered counsel.

Chapter One Questions:

1. What should be considered when seeking Christian counseling? Why?

2. According to the author, how we view God is the key in determining how we find solutions to our problems. Do you agree/disagree? Why?

3. What can Christian Counseling offer non-Christians who come for counseling?

Chapter Two

Basic Counseling Skills & Techniques

"But the wisdom from above is first pure, then peaceable, gentle, accommodating, full of mercy and good fruit, impartial, and not hypocritical." (James 3:17 NET)

The goal of the Christian counselor is to help the client in the healing process, through Scripture, prayer, and spiritual maturity. There are several skills and characteristics that can be found in a spiritually mature Christian counselor, such as the ability to communicate, listening with empathy, and provide competent Christian counseling. First Thessalonians 5:14-18 provides the Christian counselor with biblically core skills, to guide them, so they can become more effective. Similarly, he or she should skillfully encourage, comfort, correct, and advise the client, like the Holy Spirit does for the believer. This author acknowledges the fact that counseling, psychotherapy, and cognitive-behavioral therapy, are rooted in clinical research and theories. However, the objective of this chapter is to briefly discuss the necessary skills the Christian counselor must develop in order to become an effective counselor.

There are many skills and techniques that are required for effective counseling. These core skills provide the fundamental basis for learning throughout life, working effectively, and handling problems. These skills are generally gained through technological advancement, extensive knowledge/training, spiritual gifts, or advanced core competencies. Sir Francis Bacon was the first person attributed to the phrase "Knowledge is Power," when he published the maxim in his book, <u>Meditationes Sacrae, and Human Philosophy</u>. And knowing knowledge is the key to power, we now know the truth. And knowing the truth is what will set us free (John 8:32).

Also, a truly effective Christian counselor integrates all aspects of competent counseling practice by skillfully developing a Christ-centered model. The best Christian counselors in the field are not necessarily those who are most well-known but rather those who are always reaching toward godliness and flat out working harder than everyone else. The heart of effective Christian counseling is knowing how to use your skills and techniques to create the right spiritual environment, one that facilitates lasting change and transformation. These core skills are generally learned and developed through learned behaviors and cultural norms. Some of those developmental skills include communication, continuous learning, ability to empower, ability to engage multiculturally, and ability to adapt.

EFFECTIVE COMMUNICATOR

Anyone in a helping profession such as therapists, clinical counselors, Christian counselors, pastors, and others, needs to develop effective communication skills. Most, if not all, would agree that effective communication is a fundamental skill for every counselor. Effective communication sounds like it should be instinctive, but most often than not it is the complete opposite. For most of us, communicating effectively requires learning an important skill which is typically taught to us through formal education. However, communication is more than just the words we use. It is the vehicle in which we are perceived.

Effective communication combines a set of four crucial skills: engaged listening, nonverbal communication, managing stress at the moment, and asserting yourself in a respectful and trustworthy manner. The communication process involves verbal and nonverbal expressions to encourage the client to share his or her story. We can improve our communication skills as Christian counselors, by knowing our very words and gestures can help the counselee overcome their problems and move closer to wholeness. We can also increase the quality of our Christian relationships by keeping in mind that our words and counseling techniques are supported by God's Word. Basically, this author is stating, if we communicate the word of God more effectively, it will allow us to be more successful in counseling as well as in ministry.

ACTIVE AND EMPATHIC LISTENER

Effective Christian counseling requires the counselor to be an active and empathetic listener. Empathy is an understanding of the emotional feelings of others. We must be kind to one another, tenderhearted, forgiving one another, even as God for Christ's sake hath forgiven us (Ephesians 4:32). Active empathic listening is an activity of listening that combines traditional active listening procedures with the element of empathy which will result in a higher form of listening.

In the first years of everyone's life, we learn to pay attention, listen, and learn because these tools are important for our social development. They are fundamental skills that every Christian counselor should bring to the table. In my opinion, empathic listening in counseling is the key to a healthy and productive relationship between the counselor and the counselee. These two treasures (empathy and listening) are like the master key to the client's heart and soul, which the Christian counselor can use to enter and help from within. Among its benefits, empathic listening builds trust and respect, allows the client to release their emotions, encourages dialogue, and creates a safe environment that is conducive to combined problem-solving.

ETHICAL AND TRUSTWORTHY

The Christian counselor must establish an open, ethical, and trustworthy relationship with the counselee. The Christian counselor must develop a lifestyle of moral value in addition to emotional sensitivity, cultural awareness, balanced life, and professional competency. We are called to be reliable, ethical, and trustworthy, not compromising or conniving. If the counselee does not have confidence in their relationship with the counselor, they are less likely to be open to discussing their problems. If the counselee begins to question your integrity, he or she may also question God's ability to transform their life. We do not want any client to ever question God because of the counselor's incompetence.

In short, Christian counseling, at its best, is a Spirit-led process of change, transformation, and growth, geared to help the counselee mature in Christ by the skillful combination of Godly counsel, integrity, accountability, and spiritual interventions. Also, Christian counselors are dedicated to Jesus Christ as their "first love," and subsequently to excellence in client service, to ethical integrity in practice, and to respect everyone you counsel.

SPIRITUAL MATURITY

The Christian counselor must be a student of God's Word because Christian counseling involves the therapeutic application of empathetic listening, discernment, practical knowledge, and the careful application of the Word of God directly or indirectly to every situation presented to the counselor. Competent Christian counseling demands that we move beyond simple sin management, behavior modifications, or coddling methods. We need to tap into our God-given talent, which is the Holy Spirit, so we can effectively counsel, minster, and transform lives and minds. Colossians 3:16 reminds us, "Let the word of Christ dwell in you richly in all wisdom; teaching and admonishing one another in psalms and hymns and spiritual songs, singing with grace in your hearts to the Lord."

However, as counselors, we know that there is an increased number of dysfunctional and emotionally hurt people in our society and churches. As Christians, we must be able to counsel and provide answers through the Word of God. However, most pastors and churches today are caught between the growing epidemic of difficult psychological problems for which they do not have clear biblical answers. Another counseling barrier is language and other multicultural issues. Unfortunately, we have become a society of people who rate and analyze according to race, ethnicity, sexual orientation, education, and social status. As a Christian counselor, spiritual maturity and knowing the Word of God will/should help nullify any of these stereotypes.

Chapter Two Questions:

1. Why is it important to find out what training or skills a Christian counselor has before you begin counseling?

_____

_____

_____

_____

_____

2. Can you think of any additional techniques the Christian counselor must possess? Explain.

_____

_____

_____

_____

_____

Chapter Three

Change Your Mindset, Transform Your Life

"You were taught, with regard to your former way of life, to put off your old self, which is being corrupted by its deceitful desires; to be made new in the attitude of your minds; and to put on the new self, created to be like God in true righteousness and holiness." (Ephesians 4:22-24 NIV)

If you are struggling with the ugliness of sin in your own life–whether that is yelling at your kids or your spouse, holding a grudge, resistance to change, or drowning your sorrows in alcohol, drugs, or sex, rest assured, there is hope in Jesus. If you accept Jesus Christ as your Lord and Savior, you become a new creation in Him. The old "me" is forgiven; behold, the new creation is something entirely different

(2 Corinthians 5:7). That is exactly what Christian Counseling is about. It is an avenue that leads the client to redemption (wholeness). All the counselee's old dreams, ideas, agendas and purposes have ceased to exist and have been replaced by Christ's ideas and agendas and purposes in an entirely new creature called "Christian."

Christian counseling is a unique form of psychology that seeks to develop a distinctly Christian model for understanding the human condition. It represents one of several ways that Christians have attempted to think about the connection between Christianity and psychology. For example, some psychologists view Christianity as a crutch for weak people to lean on or something obsolete because of our advanced understanding of the human mind. Some Christians view psychology as unnecessary because all we need to know about the human mind and spirit is found in the Bible. In my opinion, religion, science, and psychology have all been at odds with each other because all three have different ways of looking at God and man. I argue God is the author of faith (Christianity), the creator of the entire universe (science), and He is omniscient (psychology).

BEHAVIOR THERAPY

Behavior therapy or behavioral psychotherapy is a broad term referring to clinical psychotherapy that uses techniques obtained from behaviorism. It focuses on directly observable behavior, learning experiences that promote change, specifically tailored treatment plans, and attentive assessment and evaluation. There is strong evidence for the effectiveness of behavioral therapy as it has been able to treat a wide range of psychological disorders since its origin in the 1950s and early 1960s. For the diverse range of mental health conditions and needs, there are many different types of behavior therapies available (e.g., Social Learning Theory, Cognitive Behavioral Therapy, Classical Conditioning, Aversion Therapy, Addiction Therapy, Systematic desensitization, just to name a few).

The premise behind behavioral therapy is that behavior can be both learned and unlearned. The objective is to help the client learn new, positive behaviors to override the unwanted, negative behaviors. "Be ye transformed by the renewal of your mind" (Romans 12:2). The Christian counselor attempts this with various techniques, including Scripture, prayer, behavior modification, role-playing, relaxation/meditation training, exposure techniques, and homework assignments. For example, if a client has difficulty identifying or attempts to alter negative thoughts and behavior, the Christian counselor might focus on addressing behaviors such as avoidance, withdrawal, or poor social skills. On the other hand, if such behaviors are not as noticeable, the Christian counselor may focus on altering unrealistic thinking such as overgeneralizing, emotional reasoning, polarized thinking, or depression.

There are three basic underlying assumptions to Behavior Therapy: (1) Human behavior is governed by basic learning principles; (2) Humans are neither good nor evil; they are shaped by their environment; and (3) All people are capable of modifying behaviors under the right circumstance. The Christian counselor's goal is to help the counselee identify any behaviors that are inconsistent with God's teachings, so they can become more accepting of God's will – even when it is not their will.

Behavior therapy is not just limited to the counseling/psychology field, it is also heavily adopted in most educational settings and curriculums (e.g., Aaron T. Beck's Cognitive Behavior Therapy (CBT), Jean Piaget's Theory of Cognitive Behavior, Ivar Lovaas and Robert Koegel's Applied Behavior Analysis). In addition, cognitive behavior curricula provide instructional techniques such as explicit teaching and use of modeling, role-playing, feedback, and reinforcement.

Numerous studies demonstrate that teaching children cognitive strategies can strengthen pro-social behavior and decrease maladaptive behaviors like hyperactivity, withdrawal, disruption, and passive aggression. In a nutshell, by using behavior therapy within the classroom, the educator can equip the students with the skills to remain in control of their behavioral choices in a variety of settings, even when their parents or guardians are not around.

BEHAVIOR THERAPY AND CHRISTIAN COUNSELING

God's opinion of us makes all the difference and has the potential to change all the dynamics that plague our natural mind with insecurities, rejection, depression, and fear. Our view of emotional disaster changes from this perspective as we are continually reminded that God is working everything for the good of those who are called according to His purpose. Compared to a school of thought focused on the idea that we learn from our environment, which is the goal of most behavioral therapies, for the Christian Counselor the purpose of treatment is to reveal a new source of absolution for those who are in Christ. Therefore, the ultimate purpose of Christian counseling is to show the counselee how to love God with all thy heart, mind, and soul because their transformation depends on it.

Some behavioral techniques have compared some of the teachings of Jesus to contemporary cognitive behavior therapies (CBT). Many behavioral therapists have also recognized the healing potential of religious belief. If combined, CBT and Christianity offer Christian counselors an authoritative, practical, and comprehensive resource for counseling clients with an allegiance to the Christian faith. This innovative treatment approach compares the teachings of Jesus to contemporary cognitive therapies, describing a variety of successful assessment and treatment approaches with the counselee, by incorporating biblical principles into logical thinking and committed behavioral modifications.

Chapter Three Questions:

1. Why is change so hard? According to the author, if the counselee allows God to transform his/her mindset then their life will be transformed.

_____

_____

_____

_____

_____

_____

2. Why do you think change/transformation is an essential part of the healing process?

_____

_____

_____

_____

_____

3. Provide at least five (5) Scriptures that prove God will and can transform your mind.

_____
_____
_____
_____
_____

Chapter Four

Counseling in Times of Trouble

"God is our refuge and strength, an ever-present help in trouble. Therefore we will not fear, though the earth give way and the mountains fall into the heart of the sea, though its waters roar and foam and the mountains quake with their surging." (Psalm 46:1-3 NIV)

The Christian counselor deals with a variety of emotional, behavioral, and social issues. None is more prevalent in the hour we find ourselves. When I began writing this book (July of 2020) the country was engulfed in social and political unrest. A multicultural coalition has been passionately protesting unsafe police practices, over-policing in minority communities, and unfair treatment of minority residents. This same passion for change and wantedness is found in most people. So, responding the wrong way, whether by pushing back at the client or withdrawing, can easily derail the client's progress. So, Christian Counseling equips the counselee with new ways to cope with these situations. It helps with feelings of depression, fear, anger, anxiety, and panic. It also can give you the necessary tools to help fight low self-esteem, suicidal thoughts, addictions, and family issues.

Major changes can come in various forms. They can include starting or losing a job, change of residence, starting or ending a relationship, losing a loved one, or even legal issues. Depending on the type of transition and how the individual copes with the change in general, major life adjustments can lead to significant anger, stress, and depression. For most Americans, the presidential election results brought not just anxiety and fear, but uncertainty for their future. During an emotional and social period like this, the Christian counselor needs to remind the counselee that ultimately its God's will, and subsequently, their strong feelings and emotions will eventually succumb to God's plan for their life. Therefore, the counselee must refrain from consequential or negative behavior that could have long-lasting implications. If he or she feels they have suffered an emotional or physical loss, they should give their life to Christ for healing (John 10:10).

This promise of Jesus may seem like a dream to many people. But these words of Jesus, spoken from the Gospel of John reveal a gift that is offered to all of us, especially in a Christian counseling setting. Also, we know that John is not talking about material abundance (e.g., huge house, wealth, fancy cars, gorgeous women/men), but abundant life in God's love, mercy, and healing. But how often do people ask for this gift? Or seek godly counseling for this abundant gift? This reminds me of the sound doctrinal teaching that I have been taught (gifted with) at Integrity Deliverance Ministry. Even as my fingertips press the keys of my laptop, my spirit hears my Pastor, Joseph Brown, instructing through the words of the Prophet Hosea "My people are destroyed because of their lack of knowledge" (Hosea 4:6).

Right now, the biggest concern for most Americans is the coronavirus (COVID-19). COVID-19 has created a contradiction in the medical and mental health field. Before COVID-19 we were told, if you need help, if you feel depressed or if you are unable to cope with problems, seek medical attention or mental health services. Now, wide scale social distancing redefines mental help as people in need of support for anger, anxiety, and depression, but because in-person treatment is harder to access, please stand by. The past several weeks, though, have wrought a change in the national mental health care landscape. A huge shift in services and social safety nets are available because of virtual and teletherapy technology. My services, "Essential Tools Counseling," being among them.

HOPE: HELPING OUR PEOPLE EXCEED

Too often we strive for normalcy, and in doing, we downplay the calling God has placed over our lives. Imagine a life in which you strive to exceed beyond the struggles and racial animosity your parents and grandparent faced. Imagine a life that exceeds your friends, teachers, and your loved one's imaginations. Now imagine a future where you experience the freedom and desire to do what you are currently struggling to do. That is the purpose of hope in Christian counseling. Most know hope to mean, having a strong desire or expectation for something to happen in your favor or best interest. However, in the Christian counseling setting, hope is the expectation of what God has promised and ordained over your life.

In July of 2020, my wife and I started a virtual awareness campaign called H.O.P.E (Helping Our People Exceed) to help bring awareness, knowledge, and vital resources to black and underprivileged communities. Through Zoom and Facebook live, we were able to preside over several informative panel discussions to help the people of God address and overcome issues, apply community and church-based recommendations, and transform their lives. Life changes and expectations can only be exceeded when there is a clear understanding of what God's expectations are of you. Once we learn to live a life that is Christ-centered, then we will understand how we can glorify God in all things and be hopeful in all things. In this way, we can lead a purposeful and hope driven life for God, exceeding all earthly expectations.

As a Christian counselor, I instruct my clients to rejoice in their hope, even in the midst of adversity and tribulations. (Romans 12:12). For it is by hope we are saved (Romans 8:24) and never put to shame (Romans 5:5). Also, hope allows us to soar beyond our past, our mistakes, our naysayer, and even our fears. It is not normalcy, nor is it some fairytale or lie. Hope is God's very promise, even before we were conceived, that we would spend eternity with him. (Titus 1:2). Now that is an expectation worth the fight.

Chapter Four Question:

1. The author briefly discussed political and social uprising in America. How can Christian counselors and church leaders help address this matter?

_____

_____

_____

_____

_____

2. How can you help people with their social and emotional problems? What type of treatments would you recommend?

_____

_____

_____

_____

_____

3. Provide at least three (3) Scriptures that will encourage a client during the times of trouble.

_____

_____

_____

_____

_____

Chapter Five

Rekindle the Passion in your Marriage

"Dear friends, let us love one another, for love comes from God. Everyone who loves has been born of God and knows God. Whoever does not love does not know God, because God is love." (1 John 4:7-8 NIV)

The Bible has a high view of marriage. It is to be a lifelong plan, not a convenience that can be disposed of in a courtroom. Christian counseling affirms that the purpose, motivation, and longevity of marriage does not come from within a man or woman, but from God. The love of husband and wife is, at its best, a testimony of the deep love between "one flesh" and God (Matthew 19:4-6). When counseling, the Christian counselor must approach marriage counseling as a covenant, a relationship based on promises and commitment, not feelings- though love and intimacy are heavily involved. A good marriage is built on oneness, emotional and physical intimacy, and accountability. In other words, if you are hoping to improve your physical relationship, you need to first work on your spiritual and emotional connection. Focus on meeting your spouse's needs and passions spiritually and lovingly.

Intimacy (passion) takes many forms in the marriage relationship: sexual, spiritual, emotional, and physical. Close to what seems to be the primary force that unites suffering to passion, the meaning "suffer" and in this sense "passion" is used in Acts 1:3, "to whom he also showed himself alive after his passion. Also, Scripture reinforces that God made man a triunity with a body, soul, and spirit (1 Thessalonians 5:23; Hebrews 4:12), and each of these must be refined to develop intimacy in marriage. This intimacy must mirror the closeness that Jesus established between himself and His church. And this only occurs when both the husband and wife surrender their lives and relationship to the Lord. Through counseling, the Christian counselor instructs the couple how to live out their marriage relationship according to God's commandments.

Another component of a successful marriage is love. Love is an intense feeling of deep affection, a great interest, and pleasure in something, a person or thing. According to Apostle Paul, "Love bears all things, believes all things, hopes all things, endures all things" (1Corinthians 13:7). Similarly, Robert J. Sternberg's "Triangular Theory of Love," suggests that love can be understood in terms of three components and each component manifests a different aspect of love. Sternberg's three components are: (a) intimacy encompassing the feelings of closeness, connectedness, and bondedness experienced in loving relationships; (b) passion encompassing the drive that leads to romance, physical attraction, and sexual consummation; and (c) decision/commitment encompassing, in the short term, the decision that one loves another, and in the long term, the commitment to maintain that love. Sternberg suggests the amount of love a couple may experience depends on the absolute strength of the three components and the kind of love a couple will experience depends on their strengths relative to each other.

In comparison, the Christian counselor suggests the amount of love a couple will experience depends on the absolute strength of the three components of a Christ-centered marriage: a mutual devotion to Jesus Christ (Philippians 4:8-9); practice humility (Matthew 11:29); and practice forgiveness (Ephesians

4:32). When the marriage maintain God's order, fellowship and passion will flourish and 1 Corinthians 13 becomes the bedrock upon which their marriage is founded. Husbands, in the same way, must pray, honor, and show love for his wife because she is a fellow heir of the grace of life. A failure to do so will hinder your prayers (1 Peter 3:7).

TRIANGULAR THEORY OF LOVE

The "Triangular Theory of Love" explains the topic of love in an interpersonal relationship. Psychologist Robert Sternberg's theory describes various types of love based on three distinctive elements: intimacy encompassing the feelings of closeness, connectedness, and bondedness experienced in loving relationships; passion encompassing the drives that lead to romance, physical attraction, and sexual consummation; and decision/commitment encompassing, in the short term, the decision that one loves another, and in the long term, the commitment to maintain that love.

The three components of love generate eight possible kinds of love when considered in combination. The three components of love work together differently in different kinds of love. However, Sternberg suggests it is important to realize that these kinds of love are, in fact, limiting cases. The eight possible kinds of love, when considered in combination, are:

- Nonlove – The relationship is absent of all three components of love.

- Liking – Relationship experiences only the intimacy component of love without the passion and decision/commitment components of love.

- Infatuation – Relationship experiences the passion components of love without the presence of any of the other components of love.

- Empty love – Emerges when the couple is committed to relational love without the presence of both the intimacy and passion components of love.

- Romantic love – Relationship experiences a combination of the intimacy and passion components of love.

- Companionate love – Relationship experiences a combination of the intimacy and decision/commitment components of love. For example, a couple feels closeness and commitment.

- Fatuous love – Relationship experiences the combination of the passion and decision/commitment components of love without the presence of the intimacy component of love.

- Consummate love (complete love) – Relationship experiences the full combination of all three components of love.[1]

THE COLOR WHEEL MODEL OF LOVE

"The Color Wheel Model of Love" theory was developed by John A. Lee in his 1973 book entitled, <u>The Colors of Love</u>. According to Lee's theory, different individuals approach love relationships in different ways. In his book, Lee proposed the idea that there are six types of interpersonal love. The three primary types of love; Eros (Red), Ludus (Blue), and Storge (Yellow), are said to be your style of love, while the three secondary types of love; Pragma (Green), Mania (Violet), and Agape (Orange), mimic how an individual act in regards to their feelings. Lee's six types of love are:

- Eros (erotic or passionate) – A passionate physical and emotional love based on beauty and attractiveness. Eros lovers are passionate and romantic.

- Ludus (sport or play) – A love that is played as a game, sport, or conquest.

- Storge (friendship) – An affectionate love that slowly develops over time.
- Pragma (practical) – A love that is driven by practicality and logic. Pragma love is non-emotional and is based on personal criteria such as level of education, religious belief, or social status.

- Mania (frenzy or hectic) – A highly volatile or obsessive love.

- Agape (divine or spiritual) – Agape love is considered the purest and truest form of love. It is selfless, spiritual, unconditional love.[2]

ENHANCING MARITAL INTIMACY THROUGH FACILITATING COGNITIVE SELF-DISCLOSURE

Edward Waring proposed that the way to build intimacy is through self-disclosure (being upfront and honest). Waring suggests increasing a couple's cognitive self-disclosure is a significant way to increase their level of intimacy. The assumption is made that facilitating cognitive self-disclosure will increase intimacy with subsequent improvement of neurotic symptoms and the couple's ability to cope with the demands of a normal social environment. Waring defined intimacy along eight dimensions. They are:

- Conflict resolution – How easily the couple can resolve conflicts.

- Affection – The degree of emotional closeness the couple expresses.

- Cohesion – Both the husband and wife are committed to the marriage.

- Sexuality – Husband and wife express, communicate, and fulfill their sexual needs in the marriage.

- Identity – The couple's level of self-esteem and self-confidence.

- Compatibility – Degree in which the couple can effectively live and interact together.

- Autonomy – Couple becomes independent of their families.

- Expressiveness – Degree in which the couple shares their thoughts, belief, attitudes, and feelings with their spouse.[3]

SOUND RELATIONSHIP HOUSE THEORY

The Gottman Method is an approach to couple's therapy that includes a thorough assessment of the relationship based on the Sound Relationship House Therapy. John and Julie Gottman's method encourages couples to build "love maps" so each partner can learn about the other's stresses, hopes, dreams, and history. According to a recent study, the Gottman method can be used as an effective treatment to improve marital relationships, adjustment, and intimacy. In John Gottman's book, <u>The Seven Principles for Making Marriage Work,</u> those seven principles are connected to each level of the Sound Relationship House. Those levels are:

- Build Love Maps - Maintain awareness of your partner's world, his or her history, worries, stresses, joys, and hopes.

- Share Fondness and Admiration - This level focuses on the amount of affection and respect within a relationship. This creates a powerful change that positively impacts the overall climate of the marriage.

- Turn Towards Instead of Away - Accept bids for emotional connection and turn towards them.

- The Positive Perspective - A positive perspective occurs when the friendship of your marriage is strong. The presence of a positive approach to problem-solving and the success of repair attempts.

- Manage Conflict - Accept influence from your partner, be open to compromise, and discuss your problems.

- Make Life Dreams Come True - Create a relationship that supports and encourages each other's life goals and dreams.

- Create Shared Meaning - Couple must build a shared sense of purpose and the meaning given to how they move through time together.[4]

Chapter Five Questions:

1. What stood out to you the most in this chapter? Why?

_____

_____

_____

_____

_____

2. If you are hoping to improve your physical relationship, do you agree that you need to first work on your spiritual and emotional connection?

_____

_____

_____

_____

_____

3. If you were going to become closer and more intimate with your partner, please share what would be important for him or her to know?

_____

_____

_____

_____

_____

Chapter Six

Dealing with Addiction

"No temptation has overtaken you except what is common to mankind. And God is faithful; he will not let you be tempted beyond what you can bear. But when you are tempted, he will also provide a way out so that you can endure it. Therefore, my dear friends, flee from idolatry." (1 Corinthians 10:13-14 NIV)

The Center for Addiction defines addiction as a complex disease, which affects the functioning of the brain and body. And the most common symptoms of addiction are severe loss of control, continued use despite serious consequences, preoccupation with using, failed attempts to quit, tolerance, and withdrawal. Addiction may involve the use of substances such as alcohol, opioids, cocaine, nicotine, sex, or behaviors such as gambling and pornography. Often, alcoholics and other addicts are the last ones to know that they have a problem because they cannot see the outwards signs of addiction. And in most cases, the addict refuses to acknowledge they even have an addiction.

Over time, addictions can seriously interfere with a person's daily life. Addiction can also lead to permanent health complications, bankruptcy, and serious legal consequences like incarceration. That is why it is important to catch an addiction during the initial stages. Statistics confirm the two most well-known addictions are to drugs and alcohol. And for sidebar conversation, they are also among the top five leading causes of deaths in the United States. And to nail the nail in the coffin, nearly 1 in 10 Americans have an addiction to both alcohol and drugs. Please let that sink in!

Most experts suggest that addiction is a disease that is either hereditary, incurable, or lifelong. Three key characteristics label it as a disease. First, it can be characterized by frequent relapses and a common set of behavioral changes. Second, genetics plays a vital role in determining who is at risk. Finally, there are effective medications that help to treat and decrease drug cravings. I do not think it is definitive enough to solely blame addiction on genes, uncontrolled circumstances, or traumatic incidents that happened to individuals when they were youths. Furthermore, why is addiction never just labeled the addict's fault? Most importantly, why are a secular counselor and therapist reluctant to characterize addiction as sin?

The Bible lets us know; addiction is a spiritual problem (sin). Because blaming your addiction on a disease or something other than sin or one's self, only prolongs the client from true recovery, which only happens when they confess their sins and ask God for forgiveness. He or she must be honest with themselves and with their loved ones and acknowledge their sinful behavior. Because for every so-called addiction today, the Bible makes it clear that it is sin. Even though society tries to redefine or relabel it. For example, what was once called gluttony is now called pathological overeating. What the Bible calls a thief is now called a kleptomaniac. What the Bible once called drunkenness is now called alcohol dependence or alcohol use disorder. What the Bible once called whoredom is now called sex addiction.

Whether the addiction is a disease, a disorder, or a result of sin, we can agree to disagree that the topic is still up for debate. However, what we can agree on is the fact that 11 states in the U.S. have legalized the use of marijuana for adults over the age of 21 and legalized it for medical use in 33 states. Also, according to the FDA, the over-prescribing of opioid painkillers is a leading cause of people who succumb to opioid addiction. Meaning, as of today July 26, 2020, the government is responsible for allowing businesses and municipalities to profit off these immoral sins. Situations such as these only make the job of addiction counselors harder. The Christian counselor is not only battling the two leading money-making machines (government and corporations), but we are equally alarmed by the fact that the United States spends more money incarcerating people with addictions than they do on universally treating addiction.

COUNSELING ADDICTION

Counseling is an essential part of addiction treatment and recovery for many people. Supportive treatment such as individual counseling, group counseling, Christian counseling, family counseling, and cognitive behavior therapy can help people recover from addiction. However, it will be argued that effective counseling must incorporate biblical principles. Counseling people suffering from addictions is full of challenges and complexities, and because of this, it is recommended that people should involve the body of Christ in their recovery. Those who attend Christian based counseling are typically giving their life and their addiction over to a higher power, God, Jehovah-Rapha.

Christian counseling has no boundaries, no matter what the person is going through, there is always a solution in the Scriptures. The Christian counselor can provide and teach Bible verses that will help transform the client's current situation for the better. In addition, Christian counseling is distinct from secular counseling, in that it specifically incorporates spiritual disciplines, biblical truths, and accepting God's will in their life. It reveals a lot of spiritual wisdom about human nature, human suffrage, and addiction. In secular counseling, the desired result is primarily related to increasing the ability of a person to become more emotionally stable and function more effectively. However, both have benefits, and choosing either of them is important for a healthy recovery. The bottom line is to seek help, get help, and allow God to transform your life through effective counseling.

Chapter Six Questions:

1. How would you define addiction and how would you address it through Christian counseling?

___

2. Provide at least five (5) Scriptures that will help an individual overcome addiction.

___

3. Most experts suggest that addiction is a disease that is either hereditary, incurable, or lifelong. Do you agree/disagree? Please explain.

_____

_____

_____

_____

_____

Chapter Seven

Teach Me How to Forgive

"Bear with each other and forgive one another if any of you has a grievance against someone. Forgive as the Lord forgave you." (Colossians 3:13 NIV)

Christianity defines forgiveness as an act of mercy to pardon, to remit, to overlook an offense, and treat the offender as not guilty, as if the sin or injury never happened. Similarly, forgiveness is an act of God's grace to forgive and forget and not hold people of faith accountable for sins they have acknowledged through repentance. Forgiveness also means letting go of your desire to punish someone or seek retribution for an offense that was committed against you. The Bible tells us in Luke 6:36-37, "Be merciful, even as your Father is merciful. Judge not, and you will not be judged; condemn not, and you will not be condemned; forgive, and you will be forgiven."

Forgiveness is also an incredible power. Clearly when we embrace what Jesus has done for us and extending that grace and mercy to others is the essence of forgiveness. In short, forgiveness is releasing someone from the penalty of guilt and sin so the relationship can be restored. This is always expressed through acts of mercy, that is, by treating the offender (perpetrator) better than they deserve. The perfect example was when Jesus hung on the cross, he kept saying: "Father, forgive them; for they do not know what they are doing" (Luke 23:34). Even in his suffering, Jesus was concerned with asking the Father to forgive those who had falsely accused him, who betrayed him, and who crucified him. This is the heartbeat of a forgiving heart.

IMPORTANCE OF FORGIVENESS IN RELATIONSHIPS

Forgiveness is important for the growth and happiness of the relationship. It is important even when logic (normalcy) challenges your reasoning. In Christian counseling, especially when faith is involved, forgiveness becomes a source for healing, restoration, correction, and conversion. In Matthew 9:28; Luke

5:17-26; Mark 2:1-12, we read about Jesus forgiving and healing a paralytic. This miracle is significant because it shows the nonbeliever that Jesus' authority extends even to the forgiveness of sin. Furthermore, Jesus told another parable about a king who forgave a servant's very large debt. Shortly afterward, the servant refused to forgive someone else with a substantially smaller debt, but rather demanded payment (Matthew 18). Both parables clearly explain how the Word of God convicts, as well as commands us to forgive others. Because when we hold on to hurt, resentment, and anger it harms us far more than it harms the offender.

Anyone that is in a relationship, especially marriage, knows what it feels like to be forgiven and what it feels like when someone refuses to forgive you. In my opinion, people who learn to forgive and forget are more likely to live happier and healthier lives because they are not focused on or stressing about past hurts, but rather on what the future holds. God knows I would not be the man, the father, or the husband I am today if it were not for the pardon (forgiveness) my wife, my family, and many others granted me. Through prayer and godly counsel, I learned that forgiveness was a must if my marriage and livelihood were going to survive. Even during the darkest hour of my life, my pastor reassured me that the very moment I confessed my sins and offenses to God, I was forgiven.

Forgiveness is what secures (and procures) our relationship with Christ. When we accept Jesus as our Lord and Savior, we receive salvation and forgiveness. However, that is not all. The Bible also declares that we will receive justification, regeneration, redemption, and atonement. Similarly, forgiveness is what keeps relationships whole. Genuine forgiveness will release the shackles that previously had your relationship and marriage bogged down. Asking someone, especially a spouse, to forgive you is therapeutic and it is a sign of growth and maturity. It is like closing your eyes, forgetting about your surroundings, and yelling goodbye stress, goodbye worry, goodbye insecurities, and goodbye resentment.

LETTING GO OF RESENTMENT

Letting go of resentment is a healing process in which you stop feeling angry towards someone else. You no longer want to punish the person for what he or she did. Your mindset changes and instead you have a desire to understand what leads the person to offend and hurt you. Because letting go of bitterness and resentment is your avenue to freedom. Freedom to forgive, freedom to love, freedom to show mercy, freedom to put the offense behind you, and freedom to free yourself from stress, negativity, and bondage.

Also, the power of releasing resentment is essential to forgiveness, improved health, and can lead to more compassionate relationships and peace of mind. Because if we let go of grudges, anger, and resentment, forgiveness will lead to the following: less anxiety, stress. and depression; improved physical and mental health; and improved self-esteem. "But now you must also rid yourself of all such things as these: anger, rage, malice, and filthy language from your lips" (Colossians 3:8). We also know that resentment is the byproduct of bitterness and unchecked anger in many relationships and marriages. So, the only person that anger and resentment hurts, is you.

FORGIVENESS AND RECONCILIATION IN RELATIONSHIPS

Lyrics to the song *Let Go*, by DeWayne Woods says, "As soon as I stop worrying, worrying how the story ends. I let go and I let God have His way. That's when things start happening, I'll stop looking at back then. I let go and I'll let God have His way." Songs such as this let us know that it is hard to forgive someone and withhold reconciliation. Jesus clearly warned that God will not forgive our sins if we do not forgive those who sin against us (Matthew 6:14-15; Mark

11:25). It is not that we earn God's forgiveness by forgiving; instead, God commands people to forgive (Matthew 18:21-35).

In, The Christian Counselor's Manual: The Practice of Nouthetic Counseling, Jay E, Adams defines reconciliation as it relates to our relationship with God and human relationships. He says, "Reconciliation is a change of relationship between persons (God and man; man and man) that involves at least three elements: (1) confession of sin to God and to any others who have been offended; (2) forgiveness by God and by one who has been offended; the establishment of a new relationship between the offender and God and between the offender and the other party (parties).[4]

When we reconcile with someone, we are attempting to restore friendly relations so that we can live our lives with peace and harmony rather than with hate and resentment. When I counsel a client that is holding on to resentment, I let them know the final step in the conflict process is exploring forgiveness and reconciliation. In Christian counseling, reconciliation can also be described as a lifelong journey going in two directions: inward, towards self-searching and confession that Jesus Christ forgave each of us despite our faults and mistakes (sin), and outwards, towards recognizing your brother or sister's faults, mistakes, and sins so we can let go of the hurt and forgiving them, just as Christ forgave you (Ephesians 4:32).

Chapter Seven Questions:

1. The Bible tells us in Luke 6:36-37, "Be merciful, even as your Father is merciful. Judge not, and you will not be judged; condemn not, and you will not be condemned; forgive, and you will be forgiven." Do you believe this act of forgiveness is obtainable?

_____
_____
_____
_____
_____

2. In Christian counseling, especially when faith is involved, forgiveness becomes a source for healing, restoration, correction, and conversion. Why do you think this is important?

_____
_____
_____
_____
_____
_____
_____

3. Provide at least five (5) Scriptures that command us to forgive those who offend or harm us.

_____

_____

_____

_____

_____

APPLICATION

One of the best parables of forgiveness comes from Matthew 18. Jesus tells the story of the servant who is forgiven of a large debt but then refuses to forgive a lesser debt owed to him. Ultimately the servant is thrown in jail for refusing to forgive the lesser debt. Forgiveness is necessary to develop a healthy relationship with God and with others. The Christian counselor can apply this concept to their life, practice, and counseling models and techniques, by engaging in self-reflection. If he or she continues to examine themselves daily, they can be the first one to confess their faults, apologize, and, if appropriate, reconcile, forgive, and restore any fractured counselor/counselee relationship.

As a Christian counselor, I do not want to follow the typical counseling norm. I allow the Lord to strengthen my heart and my mind, and give me the fortitude to effectively teach families, youth, married couples, and the community the method of forgiveness. It's Scriptures like Micah 7:18-19 that constantly reminds me that forgiveness is an essential part of every relationship: "Who is a God like you, who pardons sin and forgives the transgression of the remnant of his inheritance? You do not stay angry forever but delight to show mercy. You will again have compassion on us; you will tread our sins underfoot and hurl all our iniquities into the depths of the sea."

Application Question:

1. What five (5) facts or statements stood out to you in the book? Why?

_____

_____

_____

_____

_____

2. Identify at least three (3) concepts you can apply to your counseling practice?

_____

_____

_____

_____

_____

3. The best counselors in the field aren't necessarily those who are most well-known but rather those who are always reaching toward greatness and flat out working harder than everyone else. What techniques can you apply in order to become an effective Christian counselor?

_____
_____
_____
_____
_____

About The Author

Timothy Ware Sr. is the founder of Essential Tools Counseling. He is married to his beautiful soulmate, Dr. Zolisha L. Ware. This life journey has rewarded him with three children, Timothy D. Ware Jr., Shantel D. Ware-Moore, Kalin D. Ware as well as nine adorable grandchildren. His ministry and counseling experiences are diverse and wide-ranging. He is an ordained deacon at Integrity Deliverance Ministry in Bloomington, Illinois. He received his Associate of Arts degree from Liberty University, his Bachelor of Arts in Biblical Counseling degree from Trinity Theological Seminary, his Master of Arts in Theology from Anchor Theological Seminary, and his Master of Arts in Psychology Christian Counseling from Trinity Theological Seminary. His book deals with many aspects of Christian counseling, pastoral counseling, academic study, as well as practical Christian living.

To learn more about the author, Timothy Ware Sr. please contact:

Website: www.essentialtoolscounseling.com
Email: etoolscounseling@gmail.com
Facebook:https://www.facebook.com/Essential ToolsCounseling

The author also partners with Fearless Transformation Center and Young in Christ Ministry.

Email: fearlesstransformationcenter@gmail.com
Website: www.fearlesscenters.com
Facebook: https://www.facebook.com/FearlessCenter
Facebook: https://www.facebook.com/youngnchrist

Bibliography

1. Sternberg, Robert J. "A triangular theory of love." *Psychological Review*, 93(2), 1986: 119-135.
2. Lee, John A. *Colours of Love: An Exploration of the Ways of Loving.* Toronto: New Press, 1973
3. Kardan-Souraki, Maryam, Zeinab Hamzehgardeshi, Ismail Asadpour, Reza Ali Mohammadpour, and Soghra Khani. "A Review of Marital Intimacy-Enhancing Interventions among Married Individuals." *Global Journal of Health Science* v.8(8), 2016: 74–93.
4. Davoodvandi, Maryam, Shokouh Navabi Nejab, and Valiollah Farzad. "Examining the Effectiveness of Gottman Couple Therapy on Improving Marital Adjustment and Couples'

Intimacy." *Iranian Journal of Psychiatry* 13(2), 2018: 135–141.
5. Adams, Jay E. 1973. "The Christian Counselor's Manual: The Practice of Nouthetic Counseling." 63. Grand Rapids: Zondervan Publishing House.

Index

A

academic study, 60
accountability, 10, 29
addiction, 40, 41, 42, 43, 44, 45, 46
Addiction Therapy, 15
addictions, 22, 41, 43
Affection, 35
Agape, 33, 34
agendas, 14
alcohol, 13, 40, 41, 42
America, 26
anger, 22, 23, 49, 51
anxiety, 22, 23, 51
Apostle Paul, 2, 30
application, 2, 10
atonement, 50
attractiveness, 33
Autonomy, 35

Aversion Therapy, 15

B

balanced life, 9
bankruptcy, 41
beauty, 33
behavior modifications, 3, 10
behavioral therapy, 15
behaviorism, 15
believe, 54
Bible, 14, 28, 42, 44, 47, 50, 54
bitterness, 50, 51
businesses, 43

C

characteristics, 3, 5, 41
Christ, 2, 3, 6, 8, 10, 13, 14, 17, 22, 25, 30, 43, 50, 52, 53
Christ-centered counseling, 3
Christ-centered model, 6
Christian counseling, 1, 2, 3, 4, 5, 7, 8, 10, 14, 17, 23, 24, 28, 43, 44, 45, 48, 52, 54, 60
Christian Counseling, 1, 4, 14, 22, 60
Christian counseling ministry, 3
church, 1, 25, 26, 29
churches, 11
Classical Conditioning, 15

cocaine, 40
Cognitive Behavioral Therapy, 15
cognitive-behavioral therapy, 6
Cohesion, 35
commitment, 29, 30, 31, 32
communicate, 3, 5, 8, 35
communication, 7, 8
compassion, 3, 57
Compatibility, 35
competency, 9
Conflict resolution, 35
conversion, 48, 54
correction, 48, 54
counsel, 3, 10, 11, 49, 52
counselee, 3, 8, 9, 10, 14, 16, 17, 18, 19, 22, 56
counseling, 1, 3, 4, 6, 8, 9, 10, 11, 12, 16, 18, 23, 24, 28, 29, 43, 44, 56, 58, 60
Counselor, 1, 17, 52
COVID-19, 23
crucifixion, 2
cultural awareness, 9

D

depression, 16, 17, 22, 23, 51
desires, 13
discernment, 2, 10
disease, 40, 41, 42, 46
disorder, 42

dreams, 14, 36, 37
drugs, 13, 41
dysfunctional, 11

E

education, 7, 11, 34
emotional reasoning, 16
emotions, 9, 22
empathy, 5, 8, 9
Empathy, 8
encourage, 2, 6, 8, 27
encouragement, 2
environment, 9, 16, 17, 34
Eros, 33
Essential Tools Counseling, 24, 60
eternity, 25
ethical, 9, 10
expectation, 24, 25
Expressiveness, 35

F

faith, 2, 14, 18, 47, 48, 54
faults, 52, 56
fear, 17, 21, 22
forgive, 47, 48, 49, 50, 51, 52, 54, 55, 56
forgiveness, 2, 30, 42, 47, 48, 49, 50, 51, 52, 54, 56
Forgiveness, 47, 48, 50, 51, 56

freedom, 24, 50, 51

G

gluttony, 42
God, 2, 3, 4, 8, 10, 11, 13, 14, 16, 17, 19, 20, 21, 22, 23, 24, 25, 28, 29, 31, 40, 42, 43, 44, 47, 49, 50, 51, 52, 56
godliness, 6
Gospel of John, 23
government, 43
grace, 2, 11, 31, 47, 48
grievance, 47

H

healing, 5, 18, 19, 22, 23, 48, 49, 50, 54
heart, 3, 7, 9, 17, 21, 48, 56
help, 2, 5, 8, 9, 10, 11, 15, 16, 21, 22, 23, 24, 26, 41, 43, 44, 45
Helping Our People Exceed, 24
hereditary, 41, 46
history, 36
holiness, 13
Holy Spirit, 1, 2, 3, 6, 10
homework, 15
honor, 31
hope, 13, 24, 25
hopes, 30, 36

humility, 30
hurt, 11, 49, 50, 52
hymns, 11

I

Identity, 35
iniquities, 57
insecurities, 17, 50
inspire, 2
integrity, 9, 10
intimacy, 29, 30, 31, 32, 33, 34, 36

J

Jesus, 2, 10, 13, 18, 23, 29, 30, 48, 49, 50, 51, 52, 56
justification, 50

K

key, 4, 6, 9, 41
knowledge, 2, 6, 10, 23, 24
Knowledge is Power, 6

L

learn, 9, 15, 17, 25, 36, 49
logical thinking, 18
Lord, 11, 13, 29, 47, 50, 56

love, 3, 10, 17, 23, 28, 29, 30, 31, 32, 33, 34, 36, 50
low self-esteem, 22
Ludus, 33

M

Manage Conflict, 37
Mania, 33, 34
marriage, 28, 29, 30, 31, 35, 36, 37, 49, 50
marriage counseling, 28
mercy, 5, 23, 47, 48, 50, 57
methods, 10
minds, 10, 13
ministry, 8, 60
minster, 3, 10
mistakes, 25, 52
misunderstandings, 1
municipalities, 43

N

new creation, 13
nicotine, 40
non-Christians, 4

O

opioids, 40

P

parables, 49, 56
pardon, 47, 49
passive aggression, 17
Pastor, 3, 23
pastoral counseling, 60
physical attraction, 30, 31
polarized thinking, 16
power, 6, 43, 48, 51
Pragma, 33, 34
prayer, 5, 15, 49
problems, 2, 4, 6, 8, 9, 11, 23, 26, 37
problem-solving, 9, 37
procedures, 8
Prophet Hosea, 23
psalms, 11
psychology, 14, 16
psychotherapy, 6, 15
purposes, 14

R

redemption, 2, 14, 50
refuge, 21
rejection, 17
relationship, 3, 9, 22, 29, 31, 32, 36, 37, 38, 48, 49, 50, 52, 56
Relationship, 32, 33, 35, 36

remnant, 56
resentment, 49, 50, 51, 52
respectful, 8
restoration, 48, 54
retribution, 47
righteousness, 13
role-playing, 15, 16
romance, 30, 31

S

salvation, 2, 50
Scripture, 2, 3, 5, 15, 29
Scripture-based, 3
self-disclosure, 34
sex, 13, 40, 42
sexual consummation, 30, 31
sexual orientation, 11
Sexuality, 35
shackles, 50
sin, 3, 10, 13, 42, 47, 48, 49, 51, 52, 56
sin management, 3, 10
skills, 3, 5, 6, 7, 8, 9, 12, 16, 17
social issues, 21
Social Learning Theory, 15
social status, 11, 34
society, 11, 42
sorrows, 13
soul, 9, 17, 29

soulmate, 60
spirit, 14, 23, 29
Spirit-led, 10
spiritual environment, 3, 7
spiritual gifts, 2, 6
spiritual interventions, 10
spiritually mature, 5
stereotypes, 11
Storge, 33, 34
strength, 21, 30
stress, 8, 22, 50, 51
successful, 8, 18, 30
suicidal thoughts, 22
Systematic desensitization, 15

T

teach, 1, 2, 44, 56
techniques, 3, 6, 7, 8, 12, 15, 16, 18, 56, 59
technological advancement, 6
tempted, 40
tenderhearted, 8
testimony, 28
The Positive Perspective, 37
therapists, 7, 18
transformation, 3, 7, 10, 17, 19
trouble, 21, 27
trustworthy, 3, 8, 9
truth, 6

U

United States, 41, 43

W

wholeness, 8, 14
whoredom, 42
wisdom, 5, 10, 44

www.ingramcontent.com/pod-product-compliance
Lightning Source LLC
Chambersburg PA
CBHW052118110526
44592CB00013B/1657